Akathist
to
Saint Nicodemus of Tismana

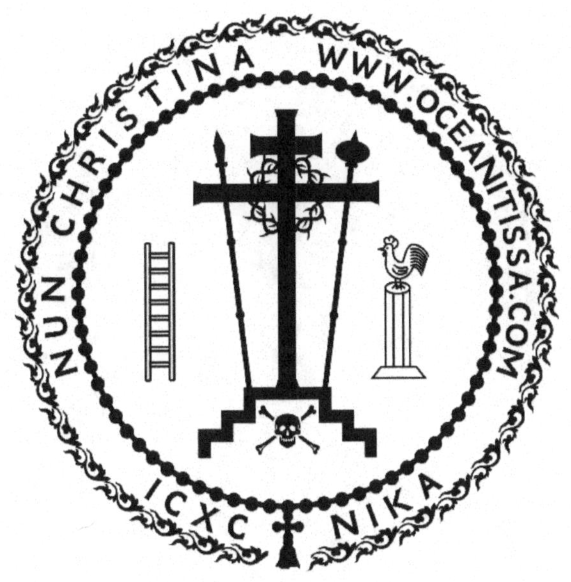

Anna Skoubourdis
Nun Christina

Published by: Virgin Mary of Australia and Oceania 2022 ©
oceanitissa@gmail.com
www.oceanitissa.com.au
Youtube: Nun Christina Oceanitissa

Subscribe to receive updates and Orthodox Christian creative
media

www.oceanitissa.com

Troparion

To the one who rose from the Virgin, the Great Shepherd, you followed like a flock of sheep, Our Father Nicodemus, you followed like a flock of sheep the one who rose from the Virgin, the Great Shepherd. Through fasting, vigilance, and prayer, you have become a worker sanctified by the heavenly things, healing the souls of those who run to you in faith. For this, we say: glory!

To Him who glorified you; glory to Him who gave you strength; glory to Him who showed straightening to everyone through you. Our Father Nicodemus, you followed the one who rose from the Virgin, the Great Shepherd, like a flock of sheep. Through fasting, vigilance, and prayer, you have become a worker sanctified by the heavenly things, healing the souls of those who run to you in faith. For this, we say: glory!

To Him who glorified you; glory to the Lord who has given you strength; glory to Him who showed straightening to everyone through you.

Akathist

Kontakion 1

We, as your servants, bring praise to you, for you have shown us heavenly and useful things, as a great protector; and as one who has boldness towards the Lord, deliver us from all hardships, so we may sing to you: Rejoice, Father Nicodemus, miracle worker!

Ikos 1

The angels of heaven praise you, Most Reverend Father, marveling at your life beyond nature; and the multitude of monks brings tears of joy to you, singing:

Rejoice, wonder of angels;
Rejoice, doom of demons;
Rejoice, heaven's delight;
Rejoice, angel of gift;
Rejoice, crown of the pious;
Rejoice, our souls' spiritual foretaste;
Rejoice, protector of your lavra;
Rejoice, guide of the monks;
Rejoice, heavenly light;
Rejoice, respite of the sufferers;
Rejoice, vessel carrying the Holy Spirit;
Rejoice, joy of hermits;
Rejoice, Father Nicodemus, miracle worker!

Kontakion 2

You have shown yourself to be a zealot of angelic life since childhood, Father Nicodemus; and going to the Holy Mountain,

you have dedicated yourself to the harshest monastic labors so
that all the hermits of Athos marveled at the flame of the divine
love that burned within you, and glorifying God, they sang:
Alleluia!

Ikos 2

The Hilandar Monastery rejoiced, welcoming the most blessed
offspring of royal descent, in whom the Spirit of God rests; and,
astonished by the power of the Grace shinning in you, Father,
we joyfully sing:

Rejoice, praise of Mount Athos;
Rejoice, mind enlightened by God;
Rejoice, lover of holy labors;
Rejoice, zealous of divine knowledge;
Rejoice, the light of the Basarabs;
Rejoice, heart full of the joys of the Spirit;
Rejoice, pleasant smelling incense;
Rejoice, giver of useful things to us;
Rejoice, along with your relative according to the flesh, Sabbas
the Sanctified;
Rejoice, for in his holy lavra you have labored;
Rejoice, for you have been a heavenly man;
Rejoice, for you are an earthly angel;
Rejoice, Father Nicodemus, miracle worker!

Kontakion 3

Being the founder of the big Athonite lavras, Most Reverend
Father, you showed yourself to be the face of spiritual toil; and
we, having you as our protector, sing to the Lord with joy:
Alleluia!

Ikos 3

Saint, having been called by God to come to your homeland and
to raise hearths of spiritual light and the garden of the Blessed
Mother of God, according to the order of the Holy Mount Athos,
you did not hesitate to fulfill it, Most Reverend; and now, the
multitudes of monks, having you as the face of monastic labors,
unceasingly bring praises to you, saying:

Rejoice, light of monks;
Rejoice, our comfort that relieves any pain;
Rejoice, sweet worker;
Rejoice, holder of divine gifts;
Rejoice, organizer of monastic life;
Rejoice, you who strengthen the hermits;
Rejoice, Father, helper of the oppressed;
Rejoice, expeller of unclean spirits;
Rejoice, God-bearer;
Rejoice, our protector of all evil;
Rejoice, most gentle shepherd;
Rejoice, defender of Orthodoxy;
Rejoice, Father Nicodemus, miracle worker!

Kontakion 4

When Antony the Great commanded you to cross into
Wallachia, you did not linger, Saint, and spreading your coat
over the waves of the Danube, you passed, Father, on the
Romanian shore, singing to God: Alleluia!

Ikos 4

Passing in Wallachia through Orăştie, you have worked hard to
build the holy monastery, Father, and Voivode Vladislav
fulfilled your wish, humbly saying to you:

Rejoice, angel bearing good news;
Rejoice, founder of monastic order;
Rejoice, for the waves of the Danube have listened to you;
Rejoice, for Antony the Great, your patron, has blessed you;
Rejoice, joy of the Basarab;
Rejoice, for they want to know you as kinship according to flesh;
Rejoice, for Wallachia rejoices;
Rejoice, for it receives you as a beloved son;
Rejoice, for you have erected a settlement of hermits at Vodiţa;
Rejoice, for God has blessed your labor;
Rejoice, the light of Banat;
Rejoice, for your spiritual sons in deep humility worship God;
Rejoice, Father Nicodemus, miracle worker!

Kontakion 5

As the thirsty deer runs to the springs of the waters, so run your soul, Father, by divine calling, to the Waterfall of the Crystal Waters, and dwelling in the cave with the angels, you sang to God: Alleluia!

Ikos 5

Father, after expelling from the cave the dragon that threatened you, you spent forty days and forty nights in unceasing prayer for God to reveal His will to you about where to raise the great lava dedicated to His Blessed Mother and fulfilling your wish, we joyfully sing you:

Rejoice, you who labored in the cave;
Rejoice, for your requests have been fulfilled;
Rejoice, lover of holy labors;
Rejoice, knower of high knowledge;
Rejoice, institutor of divine things;
Rejoice, guide of the monastic assemblies;

Rejoice, you who have risen high;
Rejoice, comforter of Christian hearts;
Rejoice, lover of God's holy places;
Rejoice, you who prepared the Holy Spirit's dwelling;
Rejoice, Father, our teacher;
Rejoice, holder of God's gifts;
Rejoice, Father Nicodemus, miracle worker!

Kontakion 6

Sitting on a stone in prayer for three days and three nights, Father, a divine light enveloped you and appeared like a pillar of fire, from heaven to earth, from which the Lord commanded you to build on that sacrificial place; and, enlightened by the ray of the Holy Spirit, with tears of joy, you sang to God: Alleluia!

Ikos 6

Father, gathering to Tismana a multitude of disciples, a great lavra you have erected, where, day and night, unceasing prayers ascended to the God of mercies, Who performed great and glorious things through you; and we, your sons, sing to you in the warmth of the Spirit:

Rejoice, Father, our mentor;
Rejoice, for you ardently pray to God for us;
Rejoice, treasury of the secret prayer;
Rejoice, pleasant dwelling of the Holy Spirit;
Rejoice, our comfort;
Rejoice, unceasing vigil in prayers;
Rejoice, the one filled by the gift of tears;
Rejoice, for you have become the dwelling of the Holy Spirit, shedding them;
Rejoice, shepherd of the monks;
Rejoice, protector of the Christians;
Rejoice, Wallachia's light;
Rejoice, lyre full of spiritual verses;

Rejoice, Father Nicodemus, miracle worker!

Kontakion 7

Through the holiness of your life, Father, you have become
worthy of great gifts; you cast out unclean spirits from those
who were possessed by them; and to the Orthodox faith, you
have brought many, Most Reverend; for which we also joyfully
praise you, singing to God: Alleluia!

Ikos 7

When King Sigismund ran to you, Father, asking for your mercy
for his daughter, who was badly tormented by an evil spirit since
childhood, and seeing her redeemed and wholly healthy through
your intercession to the Lord, with tears of gratitude, he sang to
you:

Rejoice, father of comfort;
Rejoice, pain reliever of faithful hearts;
Rejoice, the deliverer of those running to you;
Rejoice, spiritual medicine of Christian souls;
Rejoice, Sigismund's wonder;
Rejoice, Mircea's brightest state;
Rejoice, for Sigismund had listened to you;
Rejoice, for he was enlightened by the water of Baptism;
Rejoice, preacher of Orthodoxy;
Rejoice, destroyer of heresy;
Rejoice, lover of holy rules;
Rejoice, preacher of the true faith;
Rejoice, Father Nicodemus, miracle worker!

Kontakion 8

The nature of fire you overcame, Father, and standing in the middle of the embers for more than two hours, you remained unharmed, most blessed; and with your disciple, amid the flames, you sing to God: Alleluia!

Ikos 8

In great astonishment, Sigismund, Mircea, and the crowds of believers who were present, seeing you standing amid the flames without any harm, Father, and glorifying the great power of God protecting you, sang to you:

Rejoice, you who overcame the nature of fire;
Rejoice, the one full of divine Grace;
Rejoice, for the nature of fire obeyed you;
Rejoice, for you were high in spirit, staying amid flames;
Rejoice, divine mind;
Rejoice, angel with human nature;
Rejoice, for you overwhelm every mind;
Rejoice, you who humble those who tempt;
Rejoice, for all have remained speechless;
Rejoice, Father, burnt by the fire of Christian love;
Rejoice, love of the Holy Spirit;
Rejoice, glorification of your holy lavra;
Rejoice, Father Nicodemus, miracle worker!

Kontakion 9

Most Reverend Father, you were announced when the time came for your passing from this life to the Lord. And descending from the cave into the holy lavra for the last time, at the enlightened feast of the Nativity of the Lord, together with your disciples, you sang to the divine Infant: Alleluia!

Ikos 9

Great sorrow gripped them all, Father, hearing of your passing
from this life; but comforting them that you would intercede
before God for them and for all those who will ask for your help
in their troubles, they joyfully sang to you:

Rejoice, intercessor of your lavra;
Rejoice, sweet comforter of all who run to you;
Rejoice, spiritual food;
Rejoice, our spiritual strength;
Rejoice, guardian angel of Tismana;
Rejoice, sweet mentor of the monks;
Rejoice, spiritual ship;
Rejoice, safe haven of those who desire redemption;
Rejoice, our blessing;
Rejoice, escape of oppressed souls;
Rejoice, the light-carrying beacon of the Spirit;
Rejoice, angelic mind, full of divine wisdom;
Rejoice, Father Nicodemus, miracle worker!

Kontakion 10

Seeing the glorious passage of our Reverend Father Nicodemus
the Sanctified from earth to heaven, let us also alienate ourselves
from the vain world and ascend to the divine one so that together
with him, we may sing to God: Alleluia!

Ikos 10

Come, faithful, let us praise the wonderful one among the saints,
the guide of the monks and the praise of the faithful, the one in
the lavra of Tismana and the crown of Gorj, the great among the
pious, Nicodemus, and in one voice, let us sing songs of joy:

Rejoice, you who are our guide in the ways of the Lord;
Rejoice, teacher of the unknowledgeable;
Rejoice, heaven's delight;
Rejoice, star of divine light-bearer;
Rejoice, for from infancy, you have slandered the world, loving
Christ;
Rejoice, for you have taken the good yoke and the light burden
of the Lord on your shoulders;
Rejoice, expeller of unclean spirits and quick helper of the
haunted;
Rejoice, savior of the possessed child, and the unspeakable joy
of her faithful parents;
Rejoice, hastily ministrant of Christians;
Rejoice, comforter of the souls of the frightened;
Rejoice, encouragement of the persecuted;
Rejoice, our deliverer from Lucifer's perdition;
Rejoice, Father Nicodemus, miracle worker!

Kontakion 11

We will never cease to tell of your miracles, Father Nicodemus,
that you cure all diseases and, merciful, deliver all who ask for
your help from troubles. For this, we joyfully praise you and
sing to God, to the One who glorified you: Alleluia!

Ikos 11

Reverend Father Nicodemus, always putting our hope in you, we
bless you, for you have adorned the crown of the spiritual life
with your divine holiness, which over the centuries, gives an

example to the souls eager for God; and rejoicing, we, your servants, with reverence we glorify you and, praising you, we sing to you:

Rejoice, most precious pearl, the strengthening of the spiritual life;
Rejoice, crown of the pious and protector of Wallachia;
Rejoice, you who live with the devoted and all the saints;
Rejoice, heir of divine grace;
Rejoice, good concordance of the faithful;
Rejoice, chosen growth of the pious;
Rejoice, for you have filled them all with piety by the holiness of your life;
Rejoice, worker of the secret prayer, which is the sword of the Spirit;
Rejoice, you who have broken the sword of unseen enemies;
Rejoice, for you have dedicated your spiritual heritage to God;
Rejoice, burning candle of holy afflictions;
Rejoice, for all believers run to you in faith;
Rejoice, Father Nicodemus, miracle worker!

Kontakion 12

Marveling at the divine grace, which works glorified powers through your holy relics, Father Nicodemus, and thinking of the rays of radiance with which God has adorned you, we, the believer, sing with unspeakable joy to the good doer: Alleluia!

Ikos 12

You have become the image of alienation, Father, and by filling yourself with divine grace, you have enlightened everyone, and we, through you, filling ourselves with spiritual fragrance, sing to you:

Rejoice, Father;
Rejoice, Archimandrite;

Rejoice, dwelling of the gift;
Rejoice, love of the Holy Spirit;
Rejoice, most glorified daystar;
Rejoice, most glorified by the Lord;
Rejoice, Most Reverend Father;
Rejoice, we say, though holy feelings;
Rejoice, our good shepherd;
Rejoice, protector of the poor;
Rejoice, escape of the afflicted;
Rejoice, the light of the wandering;
Rejoice, Father Nicodemus, miracle worker!

Kontakion 13

O Most Blessed Father Nicodemus, receiving our humble prayer, intercede for the mercy of the Most High, deliver us from all temptation, and save us from the torment that will be, all those who praise you and sing to God: Alleluia! (This kontakion is repeated three times.)

Repeat Ikos 1 and Kontakion 1.

Ikos 1

The angels of heaven praise you, Most Reverend Father, marveling at your life beyond nature; and the multitude of monks brings tears of joy to you, singing:

Rejoice, the astonishment of angels;
Rejoice, the doom of demons;
Rejoice, heaven's delight;
Rejoice, angel of gift;
Rejoice, the crown of the pious;
Rejoice, our souls' spiritual foretaste;
Rejoice, protector of your lavra;
Rejoice, guide of the monks;

Rejoice, heavenly light;
Rejoice, the respite of the sufferers;
Rejoice, vessel carrying the Holy Spirit;
Rejoice, joy of hermits;
Rejoice, Father Nicodemus, miracle worker!

Kontakion 1

We, your servants, bring praise to you, as you have shown us the heavenly and useful things, as a great protector; and as one who has boldness towards the Lord, deliver us from all hardships, so we may sing to you: Rejoice, Father Nicodemus, miracle worker!

Prayer to Saint Nicodemus of Tismana

Holy Reverend Father Nicodemus, receiving our humble prayer, intercedes for the mercy of the Most High. Deliver us with your use, Most Blessed, from the evils that come upon us, that we may continually glorify you. You know the impotence of our nature, but you also see faith and hear our sighs; don't leave us, Father, when we run to you. Pray to the Master for us, the unworthy, to forgive our mistakes and give us pure love and strength to do all good, for the glory of His Most Holy Name. We ask you and pray to you: Father, help us because, although we have sinned at the temptation of the evil one, we run to you with a broken heart, to protect us from the deadly arrow of our enemy, the devil, who mortally wounds our souls. As you had mercy on all who have run to you in faith, healing them of their infirmities, and have redeemed the girl tormented by the unclean spirit, so deliver us, Father, from our spiritual and fleshly helplessness, and being saved by your intercession, we glorify, thank, and worship the Father, the Son, and the Holy Spirit, now and forever and ever. Amen.

Biography

Pious Nicodemus was of Macedo-Romanian origin. He was born in Prilep, in the South of Serbia, about 1320, being related to the ruler prince of Wallachia Nicolae Alexandru Basarab (1352-1364) and to Saint knyaz Lazarus of Serbia (1371-1389).

He learned to read the Holy Scriptures ever since he was a child and loved to serve Christ. When his parents wanted to see him holding high positions according to their rank, he gave up all his parents' fortune and the fame of the world.

Dressed in poor clothes he fled his parents' house and went to the Holy Mount Athos where he entered *Hilandar Monastery*.

After three years of discipleship he was tonsured into monasticism and then ordained deacon and after a while priest.

Later on he went back to Serbia where he set up two monasteries and a parish church. About 1369 Saint Nicodemus arrived in Wallachia miraculously crossing the River Danube.

With the blessing of Saint Hyacinth, the then metropolitan of Wallachia, he settled here and set up *Motru* and *Vodiţa Monasteries*.

In 1375, Saint Nicodemus was a member of the delegation who went to the Patriarchate of Constantinople to reconcile it with the Church of Serbia after a few disagreements.

Saint Patriarch Philotheus of Constantinople (1354-1355; 1364-1376) highly esteemed Saint Nicodemus, elevated him at the rank of archimandrite and gave him the patriarchal walking staff and three particles of holy relics.

He came back to Wallachia where, through divine instruction, he set up *Tismana Monastery* in 1378.

Pious Nicodemus settled there together with some of his disciples, but the number of those who would serve Christ under the spiritual guidance and advice of the wise abbot was increasing. He taught them all kindly and guided them to fulfil the will of God.

Saint Nicodemus was a great founder and organiser of the monastic life over here, according to the regulations of the Holy Mount Athos, and his disciples also founded, helped by the righteous Romanian ruler princes, the first coenobitic monasteries of Wallachia, which had also the task of opposing Catholic proselytism.

In the course of time, *Tismana Monastery* benefited from the help of ruler princes Radu I (1377-1383), Dan I (1382-1386) and Mircea the Old (1386-1418), whose father confessor pious Nicodemus was.

Between 1399 and 1405 he retreated at *Prislop Monastery* in Transylvania and in 1406 he returned to Wallachia.

Soon afterwards, Saint Nicodemus met ruler prince Mircea the Old at Tismana, who called him "my prayerful father Nicodemus", and in November he participated in Severin in the meeting with king Sigismund of Hungary (1385-1437), whom he impressed with his gift to work miracles.

Saint Nicodemus corresponded with Euthymius, Patriarch of Tarnovo (1375-1393), for defending the true faith against the Bogomil heresy.

Saint Nicodemus fell asleep into the Lord on 26 December 1406 and was buried in the porch of the big church of *Tismana Monastery*.

His relics were kept for a while at Tismana, but later on they were hidden in an unknown placed because of the hostility of the time. Only the forefinger of his right hand and his lead cross that he used to wear on his chest remained at Tismana.

The holiness of his life and the miracles he made both during his lifetime and after his falling asleep into the Lord made the faithful venerate archimandrite Nicodemus as saint as soon as he passed away from this world.

In 1955, the Holy Synod of the Romanian Orthodox Church generalised the veneration of Pious Nicodemus all over the Romanian Patriarchate, considering him as one who renewed the Romanian coenobitic monasticism and as protector of Oltenia.

Through his holy prayers, Lord Jesus Christ, our God, have mercy on us. Amen.

Bishop Seraphim (Joanta) writes of him:

When the Romanian nation came to manifest itself in the 14th century in the two states of Wallachia and Moldavia, there arose at the same time – through St Nicodemus of Tismana (an Athonite monk) – a great enthusiasm for the hescyhast renaissance initiated by Gregory the Sinaite on Mount Athos; an enthusiasm which reverberated intensely and immediately in Romania.

A hesycast missionary in the spirit of St Gregory the Sinaite, whom he had known in his youth, St Nicodemus established his rule of life in the many communities founded by himself or his disciples in the three Romanian lands. Romanian monasticism thus owed to him its hesychastic orientation in the 14th centure. The culturarl and spiritual blossoming which was its result was to continue, more less without interruption, for the next three centuries.

(Bp. Seraphim Joanta. "Romania: Its Hesycast Tradition and Culture", St Xenia Skete 1992)

Books published by Nun Christina Oceanitissa:

The collective works of St Nektarios of Aegina.
The Philokalia 5: The full text in English.
The collective works of Elder Cleopa.
The Anacreontic Poems by Saint Sophronius Patriarch of Jerusalem.
The Life of Saint Paul of Thebes the First Hermit.
The Devil: The Cause of Sin by Saint John of Kronstadt.
Faith and the Orthodox Church by Saint John of Kronstadt.
The Monastic Rule of Saint Pachomius the Great.
Supplicatory Canon and Akathist to St Paisios.
Supplicatory Canon and Akathist to St Porphyrios.
Supplicatory Canon and Akathist to St George.
Supplicatory Canon and Akathist to St Anastasia.
Supplicatory Canon and Akathist to St Anna.
Supplicatory Canon and Akathist to St John the Russian.
Supplicatory Canon and Akathist to St Ephraim of Nea Makri.
Supplicatory Canon and Akathist to St John Maximovitch.
Supplicatory Canon and Akathist to St Dimitri.
Supplicatory Canon and Akathist to St Joseph the Hesycast.
Supplicatory Canon and Akathist to St Luke the Surgeon.
Supplicatory Canon and Akathist to St John the Baptist.
The Way of a Pilgrim.
Conversation with a Grieving Man by St Dimitri of Rostov.
The Inner Man by St Dimitri of Rostov.
Orthodox Prayer Book.
Daily Orthodox Prayer book.